SUFFOLK RAMBLES
Ten Country Walks around Suffolk

Jean and Geoff Pratt

With Historical Notes

D1080520

COUNTRYSIDE BOOKS
NEWBURY, BERKSHIRE

First Published 1987
© Jean and Geoff Pratt 1987
Revised and reprinted 1992

COUNTRYSIDE BOOKS
3 Catherine Road
Newbury, Berkshire

ISBN 0 905392 85 X

Cover photograph of Orford Castle
taken by Mark and Elizabeth Mitchels

Produced through MRM Associates Ltd., Reading
Typeset by Paragon Typesetters, Sandycroft, Chester
Printed in England by J. W. Arrowsmith Ltd., Bristol

Contents

Key to sketch maps.

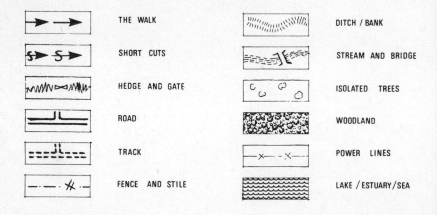

THE WALK	DITCH / BANK
SHORT CUTS	STREAM AND BRIDGE
HEDGE AND GATE	ISOLATED TREES
ROAD	WOODLAND
TRACK	POWER LINES
FENCE AND STILE	LAKE / ESTUARY / SEA

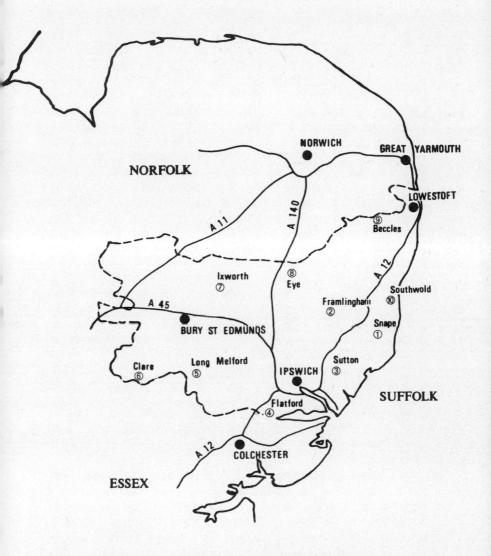

Sketch map showing the locations of walks.

Introduction

Suffolk contains a wide variety of scenery, all of it beautiful and most of it suitable for the walker, out for a day or part of a day in the fresh air. The Heritage coast in the east consists of a belt of light sandy soil, some of which is heathland, some farmland and some put down to forest, sparsely populated the natural home for an amazing variety of wild life.

Central Suffolk comprises, in the main, a clay plateau intersected by shallow valleys. The northern and southern border areas are the river valleys of the Waveney and Stour. Nestling in the countryside are the many small towns and villages, rich in history, endowed with fine old buildings, and with beautiful and lofty churches.

These ten walks have been selected to provide an interesting and enjoyable encounter with the Suffolk scene. They are distributed across the county and each ramble has its own particular charm and points of interest. Most begin at a town or village which, in itself is worth visiting. The walks vary in length but all can be shortened by using either alternatives mentioned in the text, or other roads shown in the sketch maps.

Suffolk is well served with public footpaths and bridleways. It is estimated that there are 3,000 miles of such rights of way in the country, and these are shown on the Definitive Map of rights of way which is kept by the County Council. The walks in this book all follow public paths shown on the Definitive Map except where mentioned otherwise. However changes do occur from time to time when rights of way are diverted officially. When this happens the diversion is usually well signed and easy to follow.

The condition of footpaths underfoot can vary widely depending upon the season of the year. In winter it is inevitable that there will be some areas which get muddy, while at the height of summer, lush vegetation may need to be brushed aside as you pass. Paths are often uneven and moreover, across cultivated fields they may become narrower because of encroachment of crops on either side, so for all these reasons be sure to wear a stout pair of shoes whatever the season.

The sketch map which accompanies each walk is designed to guide walkers to the starting point and give a simple but accurate idea of the route to be taken. For those who like the benefit of detailed maps the relevant Ordnance Survey sheets for the Pathfinder 1:25,000 and Landranger 1:50,000 Series are given at the beginning of each walk.

Please don't forget to keep to the Country Code; in particular, take all litter home, keep dogs under close control, and fasten gates behind you. Walking is a fine and enjoyable recreation and we hope that you will get as much enjoyment from these walks as we have had.

Jean and Geoff Pratt
March 1992

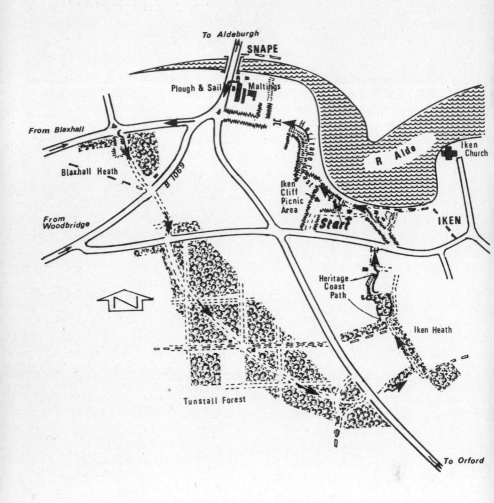

The Alde at Snape

Introduction: This walk takes you through an Area of Outstanding Natural Beauty, along the Suffolk Heritage Coast. The typical surrounding scenery includes tidal estuaries, heathland and secluded forest.

The first part of the walk follows the Heritage Coast Path. Then the route takes in Snape Maltings, the home of the Aldeburgh Festival. The path crosses Blaxhall Heath and then follows the shady glades of Tunstall Forest. The Heritage Coast Path is then rejoined across Iken Heath with extensive views of the river Alde.

Distance: The circular walk is 6½ miles in length and will take about 3 hours. It follows well used paths and cart tracks. Maps: OS Landranger 156, Pathfinder TM 25/35.

Refreshments: There is a cafe and a wine bar at the Snape Maltings. The Plough and Sail public house is close by.

How to get there: Snape is about 5 miles west of Aldeburgh. Use the A12 London to Lowestoft road. One mile north of Farnham and 2½ miles south of Saxmundham, turn east on to the A1094 towards Aldeburgh. In 2 miles at the church, turn right on to the B1069 and in 1 mile, having gone through the village, cross the river bridge and pass the Maltings. At the junction bear left and then take the next turning left to Iken. In ¼ mile turn left and enter the Iken Cliff Picnic Site. Map ref: TM 400562.

The Walk: From Suffolk County Council's Iken Cliff Picnic Site, which is on the southern shore of the river Alde, go to the lower end of the large sloping site, and turn left. Follow the hedge on your right. Beyond the hedge lie the marshes and then the river.

At the end of that field twist right and then left through a gap, and follow a scant line of oaks and a ditch beyond them on your

9

the left climbs the hill, one to the right goes down to the shore, and your path is more-or-less straight ahead, between cupressus and mahonia bushes, to follow a path, with reeds and then the river on your right, back to the Iken Cliff Picnic Site.

Historical Notes

Snape: In 1155 the Priory of St Mary at Snape was founded. In 1525 the Priory was dissolved by Cardinal Wolsey, who gave the land to the school he had founded in Ipswich. The Priory remains lie under Chapel Field. Excavators found, in 1862, a cemetery and the remains of a 48 foot long clinker-built boat. It is thought that the ship burial dates from AD550. In the Snape ship a gold ring, of German origin, was found. A ring such as this one, unique in England, tells archaeologists that this was the grave of a very important person, maybe, an early East Anglian King.

The Maltings: Snape is best known today for the Maltings and its association with the Aldeburgh Festival. Snape Maltings were founded in 1859 by Newson Garrett, who designed the buildings himself. The fine site alongside the river Alde enabled barges carrying grain or malt to moor close beside the maltings. The finished product, the malt went chiefly to London where one of Newson's sons, Edmund Garrett, managed the Bow Brewery.

Iken: The lonely, scattered hamlet of Iken in far-off days attracted the attention of Queen Boadicea, who came with her Iceni warriors and built a fortress there. These Iceni warriors left the name Iken behind them.

The Romans extracted salt from the river area opposite Iken Church.

Framlingham Castle

Introduction: This walk links two well-known local landmarks, a working windmill and an historic castle. Both are open to the public and well worth a visit.

Framlingham is a small country town which has grown up round the mediaeval Castle and lies on the upper reaches of the river Ore. The circular walk extends westward as far as Saxtead Green, with its restored Post Mill. The return to Framlingham leads past the Mere, a lake NW of the Castle, and through the Castle grounds.

Distance: The walk is about 6 miles long and will take about 2½-3 hours. For those wishing to curtail the walk there is a direct way back by road from Saxtead Green, and for a very short walk, it is possible to keep on the road round to the north of the Mere and then return through the Castle grounds. Maps: OS Landranger 156, Pathfinder TM 26/36.

Refreshments: In Framlingham there is The Crown Hotel and a number of public houses, including The Crown and Anchor and The Castle. The Volunteer public house at Saxtead Green is a convenient half way stop.

How to get there: Framlingham is about 15 miles east of Ipswich. It is approached by turning off the A12 London − Lowestoft road onto the B1116 at Wickham Market, or by turning off the A1120 Stowmarket − Yoxford road at Saxtead Green. The walk starts on Market Hill, an almost triangular shaped 'square' at the centre of the town and a few yards west of the Parish Church. Parking is sometimes possible at Market Hill but if you continue beyond the square and past the church, there is a large car park just by the Castle entrance. Map ref: TM 285634.

The Walk: The walk starts from Market Hill in the centre of

13

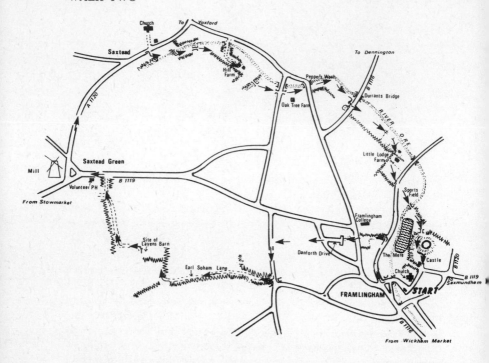

Framlingham. Go downhill from the Square, curving to the left at the bottom, and cross the bridge over the river Ore into the corner of Wells Close Square.

Take the road on your right, New Road, and pass on your left the Robert Hitcham Almshouses. Keep on until you have just passed some allotments and then turn left up a path. With post-and-rail fence on the left and the boundary hedge of Framlingham College on your right walk up to the next road, College Road, which you meet at a kissing gate not far from the main entrance to Framlingham College.

Cross straight over the road, with a pink-washed cottage on your right, and go along the footpath which snakes right then left to join Danforth Drive. Go straight ahead towards the field you can see at the end. There is a footpath signpost there.

Walk across the road and follow the path over the field ahead as far as the next road, where you turn left. As you get within sight of a road junction you will see a green lane on your right, just before a small bridge. Turn right into this lane, called Earl Soham

Lane. You will have a brook on your left. Where the track appears to go left into a field, ignore it and keep straight on in the green lane, with coppiced trees to left and right. Presently the lane comes out into a large field. The track continues straight on with the hedge of this field on your left.

At the next cross-hedge go slightly right into the corner of another large field.

Turn right and follow the broad headland path, with hedge on right, up as far as the corner of the field where a ditch lies ahead. The public footpath should cross the ditch here then go half-left across to where Layen's Barn used to be. If the footbridge is not in place go left at this corner, and follow the ditch on your right until it peters out. Then turn right, still on a broad track, along to the site of Layen's Barn. The barn has been razed to the ground, but all around the site many trees have been planted. Four footpaths meet here.

Follow the broad cart track round to the left, heading west. Straight in front of you a hedge appears to begin, and it runs to the right. When you get there you will find that a ditch turns a corner there. Turn right at that point and go north, with hedge and ditch on your left. When the hedge ends the broad track continues, passing a small farm on the left and a track going off to it. Shortly there is a hedge both sides and you reach the road, the B1119 Saxtead to Framlingham road. For refreshment at the Volunteer, and a visit to Saxtead Green Mill go left along the road.

On leaving rhe Volunteer go left again for about 50 yards and take the right fork and the Mill will be very obvious at the next junction.

From the Mill take the road towards Dennington and Yoxford, with the green on your left. Continue on this road for nearly a mile, passing a junction off left, until you come to All Saint's Church, Saxtead. It is set back from the road a little on the left, but you will not miss it. Less than a mile north-west of the church the river Ore rises.

Immediately opposite the church is a wooden farm gate. Go 10 yards beyond it and enter the field on your right by a gap by a footpath signpost, and cross the narrow, but very long, field to the hedge opposite and then turn left.

Follow the stream on your right until you can cross it by a culvert. Continue beside the stream until, after crossing a very broad cart-bridge, you are in the bottom corner of a field.

On entering that field you will see half-right a hedge. Go to the leftmost end of that hedge. Continue in the same direction across the field to join a track by a footpath sign.

Follow the track as it chicanes left then right a little, and then passes in front of the farmhouse and barn at Hill Farm. Beyond the farm buildings snake left a bit and follow the hedge on the right for another 20 yards to the point where the hedge turns right.

You are now in the corner of a vast field dropping down to a shallow valley. Before you drop down look across the valley to Oak Tree Farm, a big farm with many barns, and lombardy poplars beside it. If you now strike off across the field directly towards that farm, when you reach the hedge in the valley bottom you should come to a large single-plank footbridge over a deep stream.

After crossing the stream go half-left across the field to a broad culvert and out to the road. You are about 20 yards from some white railings where the road crosses the river Ore, not far from a road junction.

Cross straight over the road and by another broad culvert a step or so to the left, go into another field. Cross that field to another road, about 15 yards from another set of white railings. On the opposite side of the road is a rusty iron gate leading into a field planted with many sorts of trees, all in neat rows. Keep to the left in this field, with the River Ore on your left. This section is called Pepper's Wash.

Follow the river as it turns right and keep on until the river dives under the B1116 road at Durrant's Bridge which is now on your left. You keep on along the field edge with a ditch on your left, until you come to a gap by a large tree trunk. Go out to the road, and straight across through a gap into another field.

Once more follow the river on your left. Presently go over an excellent two-step stile. In another ¼ mile you will reach Little Lodge Farm. Approaching the farm strike up half-right, passing on your left a red-tiled, pale green building with somewhat unusual oval window settings.

Go through a gap in a hedge and on up to the right of a big barn, towards an oak tree on the sky line. By a metal gate near the oak tree, bear left and walk down towards a road; the castle is straight ahead now. Beside the white rails go through a wicket gate, cross the road and go into the playing field. Make your way across this Framlingham College playing field towards the castle. In the far corner of the playing field cross a footbridge and continue towards the Castle, with trees on the left and the Mere away on your right.

Enter the castle grounds by a foot-bridge, climb the steps and skirt the castle walls, drop down to the moat and take the tarmac footpath up to a turnstile – no charge for going through it, it's really just another gate. Go through and out to the road beside the entrance gateway of Framlingham Castle.

Go down the main street, past St Michael's Church and down to the Market Square once more, where the walk began.

Historical Notes

Framlingham: At the beginning of Queen Elizabeth I's reign some Statutes were introduced which protected, and enforced protestantism in England. There were many Catholics, clergy and laity, women and men, who refused to comply with the Statutes. Those people were called Recusants.

At the end of December 1600, 36 Recusant prisoners set out from Wisbech for Framlingham. They were manacled together in pairs, and escorted by 30 soldiers for their four-day journey.

When they had travelled as far as Ely, the Keeper discovered that he was responsible for paying the military escort. Seeing his profits fast disappearing he refused to pay and the soldiers went away.

Father Bluett, one of the 36 prisoners, gave the Keeper his word that all the prisoners would be at Framlingham Castle on time, and so they travelled on unaccompanied, arriving on time as promised.

The authorites at Framlingham were not prepared for as many as 36 prisoners, so for the first two months some of the Recusants were boarded out in the surrounding villages.

The Castle continued to house the Recusants until 1603.

Hitcham Almshouses: You will pass some almshouses provided by Sir Robert Hitcham, in the early part of your walk. Sir Robert, who is buried in the Parish Church, also left money to endow a school. It is now called the Sir Robert Hitcham Primary School.

Saxtead Green Mill was a mill for grinding corn. Some mills which look very much like this mill were used for drainage purposes, but were still called mills. Saxtead Mill was grinding corn right up to the time of the First World War. A mill at Saxtead was recorded as early as 1287, and this particular mill was in commercial use up to 1947, though latterly it was grinding animal feedstuffs.

This mill is a postmill. The whole body, or buck, containing the sails and all the machinery revolves. Prior to 1745 the bucks of postmills had to be turned to face the wind by the miller, sometimes helped by his horse hauling on the tailpole. Then an automatic device was patented for facing the sails into the wind, operated by the fantail. Saxtead Green Mill has a fantail.

Management of the mill was handed over to the Department of the Environment, and between 1957 and 1960 it was extensively restored.

Many mills standing in a flattish landscape have been struck by lightning. Saxtead mill's lightning conductor reaches the ground by a copper contact at the foot of the steps to a copper ring set in the circular trackway on which the steps ride as the post mill rotates.

Framlingham College facing the castle across the Mere, was founded in Victorian times. Its name around 1863, just before it was opened, was Suffolk Middle-Class College; but later it was known as the Albert Middle-Class College, in honour of the Prince Consort.

Sutton Hoo

Introduction: There is a strange feeling of isolation about the stretch of country on the east side of the river Deben, to the south-east of Woodbridge. However, it is a great area for walking, with many public footpaths across a variety of terrain. The low hills overlooking the river Deben must have been important even in the seventh century, because it was at Sutton Hoo that archaeologists discovered the famous Saxon Burial Ship.

The walk starts by passing the site of the excavations, which are still proceeding, and continues downhill to the banks of the Deben river to the Woodbridge ferry.

Then the walk runs in a southerly direction, with wide views of the Deben estuary, returning by way of the village of Sutton, the wooded area of Sutton Heath and the edge of the Woodbrige Golf Course.

Distance: The full circular walk to Sutton village and Sutton Heath is 8 miles and will take 3½-4 hours. A shorter walk of 4 miles to the Sutton Hoo ship and the Woodbridge ferry can also be made. Maps: OS Landranger 169, Pathfinder TM 24/34.

Refreshments: The Plough public house, Sutton.

How to get there: Use the A12 London to Lowestoft road and go towards Woodbridge. On the Woodbridge by-pass, and just north of Woodbridge turn at a roundabout onto the A1152 to Orford and Snape. In 2 miles, at Melton, cross the railway and then cross Wilford Bridge, over the river Deben. At the roundabout bear right i.e. the second exit, on the B1083 for Bawdsey. At the top of the hill, and about a mile from the roundabout, the road to Hollesley forks left. There is a small grassy car park on the left. This is the starting point. Map ref: TM 298491.

The Walk: Start by the corner of a wood on the west side of the

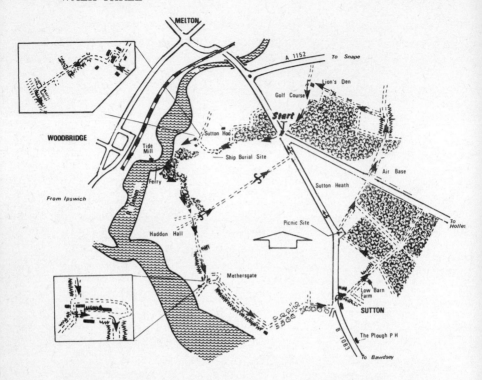

Bawdsey road, just opposite the road to Hollesley. There is a sign there telling about the Sutton Hoo Research Project. Follow the grassy path beside the vast field on your left. Cross straight over a skew cross-track. You will now be able to see on your right the white-and-brown Sutton Hoo House. On your left is the Sutton Hoo Burial Site. When you reach the entrance to the site go right, down a wide sandy track. Follow the track, dropping and curving right and on past Little Sutton Hoo on the left.

Go on round the corner to the right for about a yard or two, then almost immediately, before reaching the barns, go left off the track and continue past barn conversions on the right and later a bungalow on the left. You are heading towards the river Deben.

After the bungalow bear left, with mature hedge and fence on the left, along the track. Do not take the track on the left that climbs the hill, but keep straight on alongside the woodland on your left. At the end of the field cross a 3-plank footbridge with handrails and climb up on to the river wall.

20

Turn left and follow the path which meanders through light woodland beside the shore, with cliffs rising to the left. Soon you will reach the point where the Woodbridge to Sutton Hoo ferry beaches. This ferry had been defunct for many years, but has been restarted on an occasional basis.

Climb the cliffs from this point by a rough staircase built into the cliff, and at the top turn left, still climbing but more gradually, on a green track at the top of the cliffs, right up to the edge of the woods ahead.

At the corner by the woods turn right on a green sandy track, with woods on the left and with fine views over towards Martlesham. At the next corner turn left and later curve left a little and in 200 yards turn right at the next corner. (Not straight ahead through the shelter belt.)

Follow the edge of Deben Wood on your left, passing a newly-planted cross-hedge on the right. At the end go half-left for about 10 more yards alongside the chamfered end of the shelter belt.

At this point, at the end of the cut-off corner of the wood, stand and face across the field. Opposite is a hedge about 6 feet high. See a bit to the left of straight ahead, a gap in the hedge. Head across the field towards that gap. Immediately after the hedge you will come to a tarmac track.

If you want to return to the start, then turn left along the tarmac track and in about 200 yards, with the woods on your left, meet another tarmac drive. Bear left and go along this straight tarmac drive for a mile. Turn left onto the road and you will shortly reach the car park.

To continue the main walk, cross the drive and walk along a track, with the chicken wire surrounding a new plantation of fir trees on your left.

Cross over the drive to Haddon Hall and go on ahead through the shelter belt, and continue along a broad grassy track towards Methersgate. You can see the roofs ahead.

On this track you have newly planted trees on your right. Continue through a gap in the cross-hedge, on a broad green track still, hedge on right and with views of the river. When a building ahead, with three windows in it, confronts you, snake right and immediately left beside it. Keep straight on in the direction you have been travelling, with a farm gate and some white palings on your left, until you are right under a Holm Oak tree, *quercus ilex,* the evergreen oak. Here you will find the footpath gate and a footpath sign.

Go through the gate onto the gravel drive in front of Methersgate Hall and on past a pillarbox set in the wall on the right, to a junction off right.

Turn right along this tarmacadamed road, metal fence on left, hedge on right at first. Follow this quiet private road — but it is a public footpath — for about a mile; round the bend by Cliff Farm, and on up an avenue of mature trees to join the B1083 by the church, school and pub in the small village of Sutton.

Walk left along the road for about 250 yards until, just beyond the sign warning of deer, you turn right off the B1083 onto a wide tarmacadamed road.

At a junction of tracks, about 100 yards from the B1083, go left in the direction of Low Barn. This is a concrete track with grass in the middle, rising slowly. By Low Barn Farm on the right the concrete farm track ends. You chicane a little to the right and continue along a sandy track, hedge on left. Quite soon you reach a junction of tracks, five in fact, though only four may be obvious. Here turn left and walk along a sandy track through California Plantation till you reach the Sutton Heath Picnic Site.

If you now want to return directly to the start, go a few yards to the left and out to the road. Turn right and walk along the road for about a mile to reach the car park.

To continue the main walk, walk across the car park, from the Picnic Site, past the notice board, in a north-easterly direction (towards Woodbridge), along a slightly raised bank between heather until you reach, in about 20 yards, a sandy farm track. There is a Suffolk Coastal District Council 'SCDC' marker post here.

Turn right with a huge field on your left and heathland on the right. Follow this sandy track all the way over the heath until you reach the Hollesley road. Cross straight over this road with care, and continue in the same direction as before, with a fence, the perimeter of Woodbridge Air Base, on your right. On the left at first is gorse, scrub and a few trees, later a narrow stand of timber, and further on still, old tall trees on the right. The character of this area is constantly changing as areas are planted, mature, and are felled as the years go by.

Keep on, past a cross-paths, into a green lane, hedges on both sides. When the hedge on the left ends there is a gap on the left just before an electricity pole beside a wire fence. In a changing landscape of young trees, then old trees, then clear felling, an electricity pole is an abiding feature, serving as a constant landmark despite its sometimes jarring note.

Turn left here, between short posts which prevent vehicular access, along a track with a wire fence on the right. The track turns left, but keep straight on a narrow path between the wood and the fence. Go under two sets of power lines and come to a gate on the right on to the golf course. That is a public path, but not your route just now.

Still follow the fence on the right and further on, go over a stile in the fence on the right. Keep close to the fence now on your left until it goes round the corner, at which point you strike off towards the right of a white house called the Lion's Den.

After passing the Lion's Den you meet a cart track. Go left along it. After leaving the cottage behind you snake right a bit along a grassy track for a yard or so until the track opens out into a wide grassy sward.

Swing left to go over to the trees on the left near a corner, where power lines run parallel to the fence. Keep the fence on your left and walk on up the rise, alongside the power lines, passing Tee No. 8 on your right. After that the path curves round to the right.

Go through a small wooden gate on the left into a sandy area, where there may be some cars parked, and on out to the road at a Y-junction of roads, where the Woodbridge, Bawdsey and Hollesley roads meet, and you are back to your start.

Historical Notes

Sutton Hoo and the Ship Burial: The discovery of the famous burial ship was made just before the beginning of the Second World War.

The treasure, now in the Sutton Hoo Room at the British Museum, comprised weapons, armour, coins, dishes, drinking horns, and fabulous silver and gold jewellery. Replicas of these treasures can be seen in the Ipswich Museum in the High Street. It is thought that a Saxon King of the seventh century was buried there. King Raedwald had become a Christian; there were some Christian artefacts found, yet the Burial itself was a pagan one, a strange compromise. Visits to the site are strictly by appointment only.

Woodbridge Tide Mill: This is seen across the river, on the water-front at Woodbridge. Five stories high, elegant, with white weather-boarding and mansard roof, it stands out against the backdrop of Woodbridge town. Records show that there was a tide mill there at least since 1170. The present mill was probably early eighteenth century. It was working until 1956 when the shaft of the twenty-foot diameter water wheel broke. In 1968 the decaying mill was bought and restored. It is now well-preserved and open to the public.

A tide mill operates in conjunction with a large storage basin. The flood tide fills the basin. Flaps then automatically close, trapping the water, which is released on the ebb tide, when needed by the mill. The water drop at Woodbridge varies up to six feet.

Flatford Mill and Constable Country

Introduction: Dedham Vale, on the southern edge of Suffolk comprises a shallow valley of lush meadows with mature willow trees, beside a placid meandering river Stour. The famous landscape painter, John Constable, has captured the spirit of Dedham Vale in many of his pictures. He lived at East Bergholt, went to school at Dedham, and later worked at his father's mill at Flatford.

This walk starts at picturesque Dedham, near the mill on the banks of the Stour. The first part takes you to Flatford Mill, then upstream to Langham Church on a hill overlooking the valley. Finally the return to Dedham is through Stratford St Mary.

Distance: The full circular walk is 7 miles long and will take about 3 hours. It can easily be made into two separate circuits, with one circular walk to Flatford Mill and back. In the other direction, there is a circular walk to Langham. Maps: OS Landranger 168, Pathfinder TM 03/13.

Refreshments: At Dedham there are several public houses, restaurants and cafés, including the Marlborough Head Hotel and the Sun public house. Coffee and light refreshments can be obtained at the Dedham Craft Centre. There is a café at Flatford Mill. There are also several public houses in Stratford St Mary.

How to get there: Dedham is on the south side of the river Stour, about 2 miles east of Stratford St Mary. Follow the A12 London to Lowestoft road. Just by Stratford St Mary, leave the dual carriageway and take the B1029 for Dedham. Once there, cross the bridge and park on the right hand side of the road immediately after the bridge, beside the river. The walk starts at this car park. Map ref: TM 058335.

25

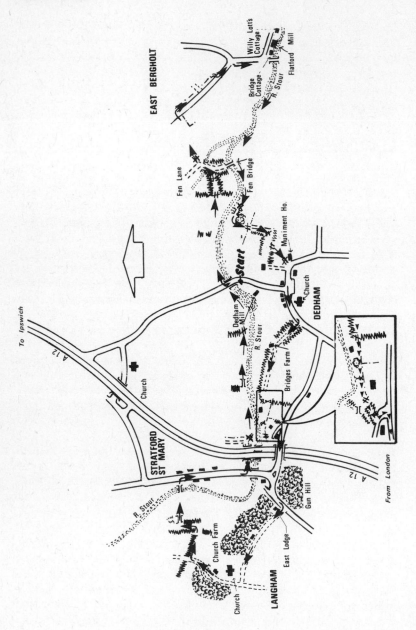

The Walk: From the car park alongside the old Dedham Mill and its millpond, go over the road-bridge over the river Stour. Leave the road, going right over a stile and down three steps to follow the river. After going through the first hedge line, more the remains of a hedge and ditch now, move away from the river slowly on a grassy track over the field towards a clump of trees and a stile.

On the hill on the left, on the skyline up at East Bergholt you will see Stour House, once the home of Randolph Churchill, Sir Winston's only son. Go over the stile and walk along a long leafy glade which eventually joins Fen Lane, in fact the two paths run parallel for the last few yards.

About 100 yards to your right at this point is Fen Bridge, which you will see later in your walk. Your route here is left across a cart-bridge over a stream, and very shortly, where the track swings left you go straight ahead over a steel stile in a metal fence.

Go right a little and in barely 100 yards cross a very shallow ditch and then veer half-left, climbing up the hill. Near the top of the hill go to the corner of a barbed-wire fence, and out to the Flatford to East Bergholt road. Cross the road and find the path which lies parallel to the road, but shielded from it by a hedge. To get to it go up the four steps, and turn right. Do not go over the wooden stile into the field.

Walk along this narrow lane, presently coming out to cross a side road off left, and again continue on the narrow path alongside the road. That path ends at the bottom of the hill by a farmhouse.

Now you must go for a very short way onto the road, the road is a one-way road, but take care as this is heavily used at times.

A few yards brings you to the landscaped, hilltop, public car park. Drop down, either through the car park or by the lane alongside it, to Flatford Mill. Before going straight ahead over the bridge, turn left along a short road beside the Flatford Mill Field Study Centre, where John Constable once worked, and on a bit further to see Willy Lott's Cottage, which Constable sketched.

Return to the bridge, and maybe refreshments at the National Trust's Bridge Cottage, go over the bridge and turn right, over the stile and once more follow the river bank. Presently you will come to Fen Bridge. Do not go over Fen Bridge but keep straight on, on the same bank until you come to a three-bar metal stile and a concrete foot-bridge under a huge willow.

From this bridge head off left across the field towards Dedham Church. At the far side of the field go over the stile and along a path between fences, with a newly planted hedge on the left. By a tiny corral go through a squeezer stile and then through a rough area up to another stile. After that aim a bit to the left of Dedham Church, and also left of the farm across the next field. Go over yet another stile and the cream cottage is your next target. The next stile, by the cream cottage, Muniment House, brings you out to the road at a bend, in Dedham.

From Muniment House go along the main village street, passing on your left the Dedham Craft Centre. When you get to the church, and the road off to the right by the Marlborough Head you are less than 200 yards from your starting point. This completes the first half of the walk.

Continue through the village until you reach the last house on the right in the old village, and can see about 100 yards ahead on the left the Hewitt Memorial Hall. Turn right off the road at the gap by the footpath sign and join a gravel drive, bordered by high trees on the left. After passing the well-kept grounds of the local water-works go through the wooden farm gate and across the farmyard of Bridges Farm, which belongs to the National Trust.

Keep straight on with neither hedge nor ditch on the left, just a field sloping away up to the Stratford road. After about 300 yards go through a metal kissing gate on the right and go on with the hedge on your left. At the corner of the field climb over the stile back on to the track. Almost immediately go over another stile and continue straight on as before. There is now a barbed-wire fence on the left, and bordering the narrow field on the right is the river Stour. You will pass along the opposite bank later in the walk.

Go straight on through a cross-fence. On your right is a small, black, weather-boarded barn. After going under a large chestnut tree there is now a metal fence, and a garden beyond, on the left. Shortly, there is a metal farm gate ahead, and to its left is a metal kissing gate. This kissing gate is definitely not for portly people!

Keep straight on. The next stile is a wooden one, to the left of a wooden farm gate. Do not go over the wide cart-bridge on the right. Climb over the stile and you are now beside a pink-washed cottage and its lovely garden.

Continue along a wide shady walk, climbing the last few yards to emerge, by a footpath sign, in front of the Dedham Vale Hotel. Turn left along the hotel drive as it curves round to join the road. Go to the right along the road, and go with it over the road-bridge over the A12 London road.

At the junction go straight ahead, signed to Colchester. You are now on the notorious Gun Hill.

After passing two houses on the left as you climb the hill, cross over and, beside the ochre-washed East Lodge, go between the entrance pillars and up the gravel drive, climbing steeply through woods.

As the drive flattens out you will be walking along an avenue of lime trees. Pass a cottage on the right, and glimpse a fleeting view through the trees to the vale below.

At a T-junction, with an imposing entrance ahead, turn right towards Langham Church. Just after Church Farm, where the track divides, take the right track and follow it down the hill. Halfway down over to the right, you can see the square tower of Dedham Church. As the track flattens out at the bottom, with neither hedge nor ditch, you come to a gap in a cross-hedge. Here turn right with the hedge on left to the end of that field. At that corner you have on your right a metal gate, and on your left a green lane. Go left into the green lane, hedge on left and the land on the right falling away to a stream.

In about 100 yards go right over a concrete foot-bridge and on straight ahead towards the village, glimpsed among the trees. Keep close control over children now, as the water you are about to cross is deep. Climb the three steps and cross the concrete bridge over the Stour, followed immediately by the sluice gates controlling the water to the now defunct Stratford Mill, and so out to the road. Within sight to the left is the Swan public house. However, your route is to the right. Having turned right along the road you shortly come to the Black Horse public house. Continue along the road, crossing two bridges over streams but stopping short before the third bridge, the one over the Stour. At this point a double wooden farm gate and a stile are set well back from the road, and there is a message 'Public Footpath Dedham ¾ mile', so turn off the road and over the stile.

In about 30 yards go through the underpass under the A12. Choose to go through at low level if possible, otherwise you will have to clamber down over railings at the far end. Ahead, when the underpass track goes left, is a wooden farm gate, and on the right a stile. Go over the stile and follow the river bank all the way back to your starting point.

Historical Notes

Dedham Vale: Flatford Mill, Dedham Vale, the river Stour and Langham Church are all familiar names to anyone who has seen several of John Constable's paintings. John went to Dedham Grammar School. From his home in East Bergholt he would no doubt have walked down the hill, and across Dedham Vale; going over Fen Bridge and then walking beside the Stour — as you will do — to join Dedham High Street at the bend in the road, and then walked along the High Street to the Grammar School by the church. John's father had inherited Flatford Mill, and he also owned a mill at East Bergholt. John worked for his father in the business for a year or so, but he spent most of his time painting.

Flatford: The mill once owned by John Constable's father is now a residential centre for the Field Studies Council. They run, at the mill, courses on all manner of country-based subjects. Next door to the mill, and also managed by the Field Studies Council, is Willy Lott's Cottage, which is seen in the *Hay Wain*.

Dedham: In the years around 1900, for a fortnight each year, the Gleaner's Bell was rung at Dedham Church at 8am and at 7pm to inform the parishioners that gleaning might begin or cease. Gleaners bells are a rarity in English parishes.

Fen Bridge: This footbridge over the Stour had collapsed quite a few years ago and has only recently been replaced. The Royal Air Force came to the help of the Suffolk and Essex County Councils. One bitterly cold February day in 1985 an RAF team, with their Chinook helicopter, ferried in the two bridge sections, each 75 feet long and weighing six tons. It would have been impossible to position them otherwise.

Long Melford

Introduction: Long Melford is a large village rather than a town.
It is certainly long. It has a memorable High Street and an equally
memorable green. Within the parish are two fine and important
Elizabethan manor houses: Melford Hall and Kentwell Hall. Both
have been restored and are open at times to the public. But if you
do go there do try and fit in this walk as well! It starts near Holy
Trinity church at the north end of the village, extends northwards
through parkland to pass Kentwell Hall. The route loops round
through the typical arable farmland of Suffolk to the Chad Brook
and then south alongside the brook and back to Long Melford.

Distance: This circular walk is 6 miles long and will take about 2½
hours. There is a short cut north of Kentwell Hall by which you
may return to the start, to make a 3 mile walk. Maps:
OS Landranger 155, Pathfinder TL 84/94.

Refreshments: In Long Melford there are several choices of pubs
and restaurants and also the Bull Hotel and the Crown Inn. At
Bridge Street, the Rose and Crown is a convenient half-way stop.

How to get there: Long Melford is about 3 miles north of Sudbury
on the A134 Sudbury to Bury St Edmunds road. Make for the
prominent parish church at the northern end of the village, close to
the junction between the A134 and the A1092 road to Haverhill.
The walk starts on the green, in front of the old almshouses, just
south of Long Melford Church. Park alongside the cul-de-sac which
leads to the church. Map ref: TL 865467.

The Walk: Leave the green, immediately south of the church, and
go east across the green, passing the almshouses and going out to
the road.
 Walk a few yards alongside the road, and then go leftish into the

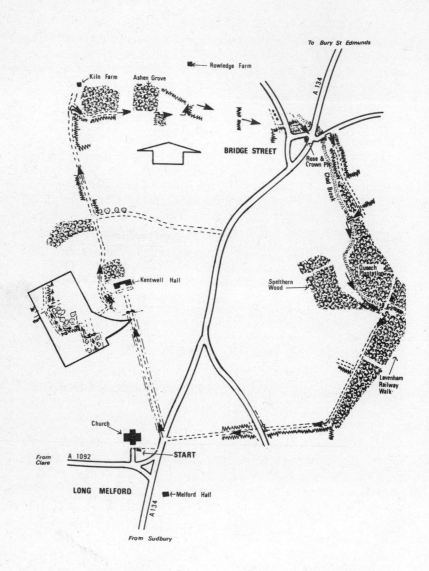

To Bury St Edmunds

A 134

← Rowledge Farm

Kiln Farm   Ashen Grove

BRIDGE STREET

Rose & Crown Ph.

Chad Brook

Quaech Plantation

Kentwell Hall

Spelthorn Wood

Lavenham Railway Walk

Church

START

From Clare   A 1092

LONG MELFORD

←Melford Hall

A 134

From Sudbury

main drive of Kentwell Hall. Pass between the massive brick pillars, with obelisks on top, and on along the avenue of lime trees, right up to the large pair of ornamental iron gates, flanked on either side by iron railings, and you are now about 100 yards from Kentwell Hall.

Before the gates go left beside the low wall topped by railings, for about 10 yards, then in the corner go through the small gate and follow the fenced path round the corner to the end where there are two stiles and a wooden gate clustered together. Go over the stile and turn right, with trees − mainly ash − on the right and barbed wire on the left.

Just after a very large beech tree on the right go to the right of a wire fence to the corner of a field, turn right and then curve left following the hedge on your left. You get closer and closer to the farm track on your right. At the end of the thin tongue of this field go over a stile and join the farm track, close by a pair of wooden farm gates. Keep going along the broad farm track, passing the end of a track off left, and with the wooded gardens of Kentwell on your right. The path curves left a little then continues straight into the distance. Later with woodland on your left you go straight over at a cross-paths, all of which are public paths.

(If you wish to curtail the walk, the track to the right leads to the A134 and thence back to Long Melford.)

To continue the walk, stay on the broad, gravelly track with hedge on right, and a sprinkling of trees both sides at first, later a hedge on right and then further on, a hedge on the left.

After about ¾ mile from Kentwell Hall the path snakes a little, right then left, with a cross-hedge off right and lots of oaks. Continue on to a point where the track divides at an open space with woodland ahead and to the right. There is a track straight ahead which wanders on between farm buildings, but you go right at this point on a broad cart track towards the wood.

The track curves round, seeming almost to be going back on itself, and you are now in a green lane with woodland to left and a hedge and ditch on right.

When the woodland on the left ceases, you keep going in the same easterly direction across the field, towards the corner of the next piece of woodland about 150 yards away, ahead and to the left. As you go you will see, half-left, Alpheton Church. Keep straight on with the wood, Ashen Grove, on your left.

As the field on your right ends the path makes a tiny dog-leg to the right and after that, on your right, is a wood. From the end of that wood on your right, strike across the field, a bit to the left of straight ahead (bearing 076°), for about 200 yards towards a hedge line that runs away to the left from you.

At the hedge go left with hedge on your right to where the hedge ends at an open space with an oak tree close by. From this point turn right (east) and look across the field for a gap in the far hedge, with a bar across the gap — the remains of an old gate. If you need to check your direction, look along a line at right angles to the hedge you have been following. The gap will be a little to the left of that line. Make for that gap and when you get there stop and consider the route.

Ahead in the distance on another hill is a church, Lavenham Church, 2½ miles away. In the near ground you can see the roofs of about three houses in the valley below. To the right of those houses you can see a transformer on a pole, and to the right of that again is the corner of a field.

Walk over to that corner of the field and then go downhill with hedge and ditch on right, towards the transformer on a pole and out over a stile by a footpath sign, to a service road on your left, just where it joins Aveley Lane in the hamlet of Bridge Street.

Turn right for a couple of yards along the road and then go left down a track, surfaced at first, then grassy. After 50 yards or so go along a fenced path, over a stile and then half-right across a small field to another stile by a footpath sign, and out to the road. You are now just opposite the Rose and Crown.

From the Rose and Crown cross over the main road, the A134, and take the road opposite to Lavenham. Follow the road round the bend for 100 yards, cross the Chad Brook and turn right off the road onto a footpath. It is actually a broad farm track, with the brook on the right and a bank on the left. As it curves to the right there are hedges both sides, and later as you leave the green lane the brook is going further away from your path. Now, still on the track, skirt some woods on your right which are between your track and the brook.

Continue along the good farm track across a field and at the next cross-hedge on the left you go right.

Cross the stream by a wide brick bridge and go left. You continue to follow the stream, but it is now on your left. Presently you will be walking, still beside the brook, with a wooded hill on your right a field away. Your route is to stick with the Chad Brook as it enters a poplar grove.

Eventually you reach a cart-track at a T-junction. At this point on your left is a ford. However, here you turn right, and in about 30 yards enter a big field by a gap, guarded by a Second World War pill-box. Follow the grassy-middled cart-track, with woodland on your left, for about ½ mile.

Do not, on this occasion, deviate to the left into the woods on the permissive track from Long Melford to Lavenham: the Lavenham Railway Walk.

Keep straight on, passing another track, this time off right up the hill. Presently you pass another pill-box, on your left. Towards the end of this enormous field you climb slightly for the last 100 yards; the wood on your left has now ended.

Your track swings right and climbs the hill, with a hedge on the left. At the top cross straight over the Long Melford bypass and continue on the concrete track that goes in basically the same direction as before. Keep on this track until after passing through a nursery you emerge on the road opposite the main gates to Kentwell Hall. Go left and make your way back to the start.

Historical Notes

Long Melford: The name Melford comes from Mel, a mill, and a ford. The mill was recorded in the Domesday Book. A few yards to the east of the new bridge, near Bull Lane, is a much older bridge. About here was the ford over the Chad Brook, a tributary of the Stour. The church is partly obscured by the Hospital of the Holy Trinity, a group of Tudor almshouses founded in 1573 by William Cordell, Solicitor-General, and Speaker of the House of Commons.

Holy Trinity Church as it stands today, is one that was rebuilt in the years between 1479 and 1496, by subscriptions from wealthy local families, mainly clothiers. Their names can be made out around the outside of the church. The church is very large, and light streams through its hundred or so windows, showing up its massive chestnut roof, among other treasures.

Melford Hall, built on the site of an earlier Hall, is a characteristically Elizabethan mansion. It is now owned by the National Trust. Beatrix Potter, who` wrote and illustrated many children's books, spent many happy holidays at Melford Hall with her cousin Ethel, Lady Hyde Parker. Some of her illustrations for Jeremy Fisher were sketched at the ancient fishpond.

Kentwell Hall: Almost a mile to the north of the village, by way of a lime avenue planted in 1678, is Kentwell Hall, another red brick, E-shaped, Elizabethan mansion.

Clare and Cavendish

Introduction: On the western edge of Suffolk, nestling in the upper reaches of the Stour Valley, is the delightful small town of Clare. Clare is rich in history, having a Norman castle and a mediaeval priory within its boundaries. The ruined castle and the river Stour are the principal attractions of the Clare Castle Country Park. The walk starts in the shadow of the castle and circles to the west of the town, passing the iron age fort on Clare Common. The walk continues across rich farmlands, to the village green of Cavendish. The return to Clare follows the peaceful river Stour.

Distance: The full walk is about 9½ miles and will take about 4 hours. The route can easily be divided into a 3½ mile walk to the west of Clare, and a 6 mile circular walk to Cavendish. Maps: OS Landranger 155, Pathfinder TL 84/94.

Refreshments: The Bell Hotel in Clare and several public houses in Clare and Cavendish. There are a number of cafés and restaurants as well. Light refreshments and teas are available at the Sue Ryder Museum in Cavendish.

How to get there: Clare is on the south-west corner of the county. From the east, go to Sudbury and take the A134 Bury St Edmunds road and at the northern end of Long Melford, turn left on to the A1092 and in about 6 miles reach Clare. From Bury St Edmunds and the north, take the A134 towards Sudbury, and about 4 miles before Sudbury, turn right onto the A1092. To reach the Country Park where the walk begins, coming from Long Melford, turn left by the Bell Hotel, pass the Square and then bear right, following the sign. Turn left into Malting Lane and in about 200 yards, enter the car park. Map ref: TL 770452.

The Walk: If you wish to make the 6-mile walk leave the car park

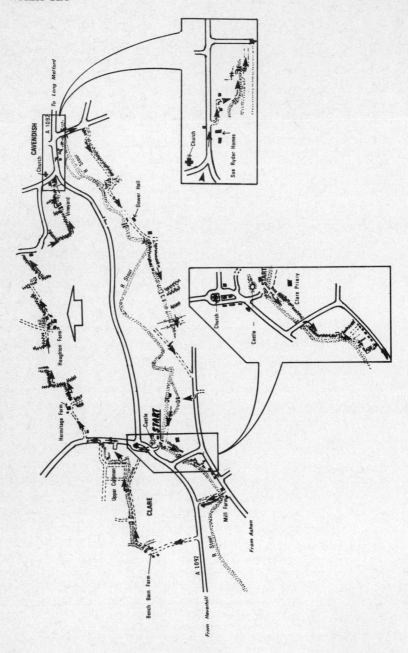

and walk to the town. Go up High Street, past the Swan public house and with the church on your right. In about half-a-mile you will reach a road sign on your left, indicating a T-junction on the right. Here you join the main walk.

For the main walk, from the car park at Clare Castle Country Park go to the south-west corner, cross the old iron railway bridge over the river Stour and carry straight on. Ahead there is the old railway track with light woodland on both sides, and also a parallel path a few yards away beside the river. Take the one beside the river and shortly reach the road, close to the road bridge over the Stour.

Go left for a few yards and turn right off the road, by the concrete apron. Pass the rear, low, breeze-block wall and follow the field edge, with light woodland on the right, all the way across the field. In the corner of the field go down, find, and cross a two-plank footbridge across a feeder stream close to the river.

Keep straight on, keeping fairly close to the river, at the bottom ends of some long gardens. Having been close to the river, and crossed the end of several gardens, enter a narrow path with fences of various types on the left, and a rough hedge on the right. This path continues generally in the direction you have been travelling, but the river swings away to the right.

Come out of the narrow path (it is about 50 yards long) and you will be in an area of rough grass with a ditch on the right and a number of houses about 50 yards away to the left. Continue in the same direction with the ditch on the right. You will see ahead just after a large ash tee, a chain-link fence behind a row of young cupressus trees at right angles to your path. Pass the end of this fence on your left and follow a narrow path with railings and corrugated iron on the left, for a few more yards to a solid wooden door in a high fence. Go through the door into a smallholding and turn left. Pass a house on the left and go out to the road, the Clare to Ashen road.

Turn right along the road, pass a T-junction off left, and continue straight on towards Ashen, as far as the yellow painted brick bungalow, Waltons. Go right, off the road between Waltons and the huge barns of Mill Farm. There is a footpath sign here.

Continue up and over the metal footbridge over the Stour. Keep on the broad track, until you finally join the road to Stoke-by-Clare.

Turn left along the road, down into a dip, and at the bottom go right up the surfaced drive to Bench Barn Farm.

Beyond the red-brick farmhouse is a row of white cottages on the left, and on the opposite side of the drive there is a red-brick, L-shaped barn. Go between the white cottages and the barn and turn right behind the barn.

Carry on up a green farm track, with a ditch on the left. At a corner turn right, on a grassy track climbing, and still with a ditch on the left. As you top the rise you will see, half-right, Clare Church, and to the right of that the castle ruins on their mound.

Drop down the hill on this grassy track. Go under some power lines on wooden poles, and just by the pole on your left is a wooden footbridge. Go left over the footbridge and continue in the same direction, now with the stream on your right, bending slowly left, with allotments to your left. Keep on this wide grassy track. As the allotments end, the stream divides and your track goes left a little, with the stream on the right.

Just after a tiny brick building on your right, go right over a stream and a stile on to the Lower Common. Initially go straight ahead towards the leftmost house that you can see; later cross at an angle a path that leads down to a gate and the street. Bear left across the common to a gap, a dip, by two buff houses with porches and brown roofs. When across the common go over the rather rough stile and turn right down a lane, with a ditch on the left, out to the road, the B1063, by a house called Brookfield.

(For those wishing to return to Clare, turn right and follow the road, keep to the right of the parish church and in about a mile you will be back at the car park.)

To continue the main walk turn left along the road for about ¼ mile, until you reach a road sign on the left indicating a T-junction ahead. This is where the 6-mile walk joins the main walk.

By some white posts turn right off the road onto a concrete track that leads to the Hermitage. It curves to the left a little as it passes a small pumphouse. Pass Hermitage Farm on your left and curve round to the right, following the way-marks with a new barn on your left.

From here you see a hedge going straight ahead climbing the hill. Go over to the double, cross-braced electricity pole near the hedge at the corner. Walk through the gap into a very large field, sloping away to the right and rising away from you.

Leave the way-marked circular walk round Clare, and follow the hedge on your left climbing up the hill. At a cross-hedge go through the wide gap into the next big field, bear left and continue on the broad green headland path with hedge on left, now heading in a northerly direction. At a corner turn right, still following the ditch on the left, to the next corner. When this ditch turns left you go straight ahead, on a field path heading for the left end of Houghton Hall.

One field further on you pick up a hedge on your left. Cross a stream by a broad cart-bridge and continue on a good cart track, with hedge and ditch on left. You should now arrive at a green oil storage tank, near the farm. At the oil storage tank follow the footpath sign and go straight on along a cart track beside a hedge on the right. Soon the track swings right and left through the hedge.

Follow the hedge and ditch of this very big field, on your left. When the ditch ends keep straight on, on this cart track, down the field towards the ditch at the bottom, then turn right following the ditch on your left. After about 200 yards on this wide green headland turn left and cross the stream by a wooden footbridge, with a handrail. You are now in the corner of a field which rises ahead and to the left. Immediately go right, across a shallow ditch, and climb the field with the hedge on your left. At the top of the rise go between a hedge on the left and the garden hedge on your right, out to the road.

Go right, past the cottage, downhill along the road to the point where the road bends left. There is a footpath sign here. Keep straight on down the hill over the field to the corner of the next field on your left, and continue on down, now with a ditch on your left.

When the hedge and ditch turn left so do you, still with hedge and ditch on your left. At the crest of the hill there is a cross-hedge on the left. A few yards beyond this point look for a three-sleeper plank bridge across the ditch on the left. Cross this bridge and then turn right and follow the boundary with the ditch on the right.

Next, in the corner of the field, where there is a footpath sign, snake right then left, keeping the hedge on the left. Curve round to the right on the path, going downhill with vineyards on both sides. Later turn left and you will have a cemetery on your right. Go over the stile; its moulded ends are somewhat unusual.

You are now on the green, in Cavendish village. Go diagonally across the green, to the right of the award-winning, pink-washed, thatched, Church Cottages. Turn leftish along the main street and pass a pond and the headquarters of the Sue Ryder Foundation.

Immediately opposite The Bull turn right into a wide drive, and in about 10 yards turn sharp left along a gravel drive. The 'No Admittance' sign only refers to going straight ahead, not to turning left. On the gravel drive go past 'Orchard Ley', and just before 'Little Oaks' turn right heading towards the river.

At the riverside do not go over the wooden bridge, but turn left and walk with the river on your right and the beautifully kept riverside lawns and tennis court on your left. Follow the river bank for about 100 yards then cross the river by a wooden bridge which ends in a stile. This path takes you out to Pentlow Lane, not far from the Railway Arms.

Turn right, cross Pentlow Bridge and walk along the road. At the T-junction where the road to Foxearth joins the road to Belchamp St Paul, turn right off the road onto a track, following a hedge on the right. After about 100 yards the track changes to the other side of the hedge. The track continues for nearly ½ a mile and then enters a narrow belt of woodland. When you come out into a large field turn right and follow the track round the field. As you approach Bower Hall Farm there is a post-and-rail fence on the right and then a hedge begins on the left; you are close to the river Stour here. Continue on the track past the farm and passing a path, on the right, leading across the river back to Cavendish. Soon the track reaches the river bank, near a barn on the left and a small brick pumping station on the right. Do not go over the farm bridge, but go on up the track. Immediately after the pumping station go right along a green lane; the river is below you on the right. At the end of the green lane continue with a ditch on the right.

At the point where the ditch on the right is crossed by a wide culvert and a broad green lane leads left up the hill, you go straight on into a small field. Follow the hedge on the right for about 50 yards. Go through the cross-hedge and straight on, with a ditch on the right. You will shortly come to a wide culvert to the right, flanked by power lines. Go straight on under the power lines, following a ditch on the right. You will soon be walking at the top of a bank that slopes down to the field on the right. Where the bank comes to an end, turn right and go across the open field towards the river.

In about 100 yards you reach a farm track. Turn left along the farm track and continue out to the road. Turn right along the road. Having passed a drive to a house on the left you will see, half-right, a foot-bridge across the river a field away. Keep going along the road until the bridge is immediately on your right, and just before some fir trees, turn right, cross the field and then the bridge. Cross the meadow beyond the bridge, heading for the left of a red barn. At the barn do not go through the kissing gate, but go left along the field boundary.

Go over the foot-bridge over a weir just by a mill. Continue on a wide grassy path, with the river Stour on the right, back to the start of the walk.

Historical Notes

Clare: Probably around AD300 the first settlement in this area was laid out. The Romano-British camp, a large double-ditched camp called Ebury is still very clearly defined. It covers a 2-acre site on Lower Common, to the west of the town. This walk crosses the site.

Clare Castle: When the Normans built the castle at Clare, about ½ mile to the east of the Romano-British camp, the centre of population shifted with it to within the protection of the castle walls. The castle lands were given by William the Conqueror to Richard FitzGilbert, and were known as the Honour of Clare. The Earldom of Clare became extinct when Gilbert of Clare was killed at the Battle of Bannockburn in 1314.

The Priory, close by the Country Park, was the first English priory of the Augustinian Friars, founded in 1248. In 1951 the priory was sold back again to the Augustinian Friars, it having been out of their hands since 1538, when monasteries were suppressed by Henry VIII.

The church of St Peter and St Paul, one of the largest in East Anglia, is evidence of the thriving wool trade of the fifteenth century, when this church was largely rebuilt. It is amazingly light inside.

Ancient House: Across the churchyard from the south porch is the Ancient House, white-washed and richly pargeted. It has an overhanging upper storey, and an oriel window. It is now a museum.

Swan Inn: Fixed to the facade of the Swan Inn, in the High Street, is a very old, probably early fifteenth century, carving of a chained swan. It is thought to have supported an oriel window in the castle.

The Country Park, besides being the site of the castle, was also the town's railway station. The line was closed in 1967 by the Beeching axe. Parts of the old station are still in evidence, the Visitors' Centre for instance.

Cavendish: The headquarters of the Sue Ryder Foundation is in Cavendish. This international foundation, dedicated to the relief of suffering, has about 80 Homes, both in Britain and scattered around the world. In the grounds of the Cavendish Home is a museum, showing the work over the years of the Foundation throughout the world.

St Mary's Church in Cavendish has an unusual feature. From the village green look up to the top of the tower. You will see beside the bell-cote a chimney. A chimney on the church tower! Within the tower is a room on the first floor which has in it a fireplace, a window seat, a window to the west and also a narrow window looking down onto the inside of the church.

Pakenham: Watermills and Windmills

Introduction: Ixworth and Pakenham are villages in the northern part of Suffolk. Like most of Suffolk, the farming here is mostly arable, concentrating on cereal growing. Perhaps this is why Pakenham has both a windmill and a watermill within the parish. An old Roman road crosses the area and Roman remains have been found at Ixworth. This walk runs in a 'westerly direction from Ixworth and then loops back southward towards Pakenham. At the windmill, a working example of a tower mill, the walk turns south, following at first, the route of the Roman road. The return to Ixworth is along the valley of the Black Bourn river, passing the watermill which is being preserved by the Suffolk Preservation Society and is open to the public.

Distance: The full circular walk is 9½ miles and will take about 4 hours. The two loops of the walk can be tackled separately, the route to the west of Ixworth being 3½ miles, and that to the south, 6½ miles. Maps: OS Landranger 155, Pathfinder TL 86/96.

Refreshments: At Ixworth there is the Pickerel public house, and along the route, at Pakenham, the Fox public house serves food.

How to get there: Ixworth is 6 miles north-east of Bury St Edmunds, just off the A143 Bury to Diss road which by-passes the village.

From the south, take the A45 Ipswich to Bury St Edmunds road and 7 miles north west of the Stowmarket junction take the A1088 road signed for Ixworth. The walk starts at the parish church (St Mary the Virgin) which is situated just to the west of the main street through the village. Map ref: TL 931704.

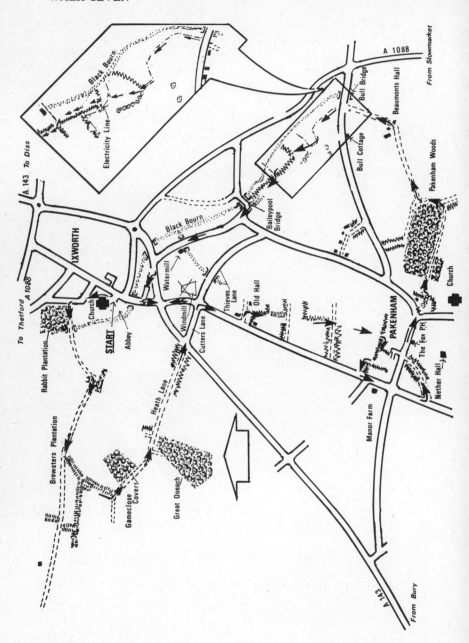

The Walk: Once in St Mary's churchyard turn right and pass the end east of the church, and follow the path out to a road.

(For those who wish to walk the southern loop only, turn right, and at the main street go towards Bury St Edmunds. At the edge of the village make for the windmill where you join the route of the walk).

Go left and almost immediately follow the bend in the road to the right. Follow the road for 100 yards more until you reach a public bridleway on the left. By a gap beside the metal gate enter an avenue of poplars. Keep on this bridleway, to the left is Ixworth Abbey.

By the brick bridge cross the Black Bourn river, pass new plantations on both sides on to higher, open ground. Continue on this farm track. Presently you reach a narrow belt of woodland ahead, at right angles to your track. Although narrow it is a long belt extending mostly to your left. At the tree belt turn right and cross a concrete/breeze block bridge and continue with the tree belt on the left to its end in 200 yards. When the tree belt ends, keep straight on, on the broad and well-used track which leads to Great Livermere about 2 miles away. Climb slightly with a ditch on the left. Pass a lone ash tree and a little later note an electricity power line coming in from the left and running parallel to the track for about 200 yards.

At the point where the power line turns to the right and a track branches off to the right, go straight on along the broad track with a narrow belt of newly planted trees on the left to the corner of that new plantation.

Turn left at the signpost (Bridleway 4) off the broad track and follow the edge of the new plantation on your left. At the next corner, turn half right along the edge of a ditch on the left, and in about 100 yards reach the corner of a tiny mature wood or covert. Cross the shallow ditch on your left and continue with the tiny covert on your left. At the end of the wood, there is a ditch on your left which you follow for 300 yards to meet a farm track at a point where it makes a right angle bend.

Turn left and go along the sandy track, Heath Lane, which has grass in the middle and a few trees beside it, to the corner of Gameclose Covert about 200 yards away.

Continue along the track, passing beside Gameclose Covert on your left. Go on with wide views and just a few lone oak trees to be seen. After Gameclose Covert the track curves left a little. Soon a track goes off to the right near a line of poplars. Your route is straight on along Heath Lane heading towards Pakenham Windmill which you can now see.

Continue downhill between orchards, still on a farm track, and eventually reach a road at a T-junction. This is the A143 Diss to Bury St Edmunds road. Cross straight over into Cutter's Lane, climbing slightly, up to the windmill.

(You can curtail the walk at this point by turning left at the cross-roads beside the windmill and return to Ixworth via the main road.)

Continuing the main walk, go right at the cross-roads, by the windmill. Do not go straight ahead into Thieves' Lane. The road you have turned into was an old Roman road. Continue towards Pakenham until you come to two houses and a bungalow on the left.

Turn left off the road along the track between the bungalow and the houses. It curves to the right a bit towards Old Hall Farm. Immediately after the pond go right, with a small paddock on the left. At the corner of the paddock snake left and right through a gap into a field with a hedge on your left. At the end of the farm garden the hedge ends and there is a tiny dog-leg to the left and you now continue with a ditch on your left. Before the field ends the ditch peters out and you now have a low bank on your left. Ahead is a cross-hedge.

Cross a sandy farm track and keep straight on across an open field, heading for a hedge corner. When you reach it keep straight on but now with the hedge on your left. Further on you come to another sandy track at right-angles to your route. Go right about 15 yards to a footpath across the next field. Look ahead across the field and you will see what appear to be four blocks of houses, each with three chimneys, all looking alike. The path leads just to the right of those houses.

When you reach the cross-hedge which stretches to left and to right, go over a stile, turn right — hedge now on right — and continue past allotments and playing field to the next corner. Go right through a gap and walk with a hedge now on the left to another corner. Turn left and walk beside a beech hedge out to the road, the Roman road again.

Go left along the road past Pakenham Manor and at the cross-roads go straight ahead, signed for Thurston and Beyton. In about 300 yards, at the end of the tree nursery, go left off the road on to a track. Follow this cart track all the way as it curves to the left, until it meets the road in Pakenham village, alongside a pink-washed building and the entrance to Nether Hall, a large late Victorian house.

Turn right along the road and very shortly come to the Fox public house. Refreshed perhaps, continue along the main street eastwards to the junction at the bend in the road.

Cross the road that goes off to the right with care. Go left a little, past a house, to a metal kissing gate by the roadside.

Climb up through parkland, with Newe House on your left and St Mary's Church on the right. After passing the tennis court on the left and going over the stile, go left for 10 yards, then right along a field path, with neither hedge nor ditch, into Pakenham Woods. Follow the broad green cart track with woodland on the left for nearly half a mile. Away to the right you can pick out Thurston Church.

As the woodland on the left ends there is a concrete area, and a small hillock to the right. Go through the gap between the chestnut on the right and the oak on the left, and go left with a ditch and the wood on your left. After slowly going left for some time you come to a sharp left bend in the wood. At this point leave Pakenham Woods and turn right, downhill, on a wide grassy track.

As you pass the several barns at the foot of the hill keep on the snaking farm track. It is joined soon by the track that has come from the rear of the barns. Keep going towards a cream house — do not take the track that goes off to the right to a group of houses. The hardcore track you are on will take you out to the road by a twin electricity pole, and close to Bull Bridge over the Black Bourn.

Cross straight over the road and follow the hedge and ditch which curves slowly round to the left. The hedge gives way to a 4-strand barbed wire fence which still continues to swing to the left. The path is well way-marked. Just by a corner of the field, turn right and cross the fence by a stile, into a small meadow. From that field corner keep the fence line on your left and at the corner of the meadow, cross a stile into a large arable field. Follow the way-marks straight across the field, passing on the left an electricity pole, to a stile at the opposite side of the field.

Go over the stile and keep the hedge on your left. Pass a wooden farm gate which leads into a lane. At the far corner of this field go diagonally left into the next field, not into the field where the implement shed is. Keep going in the same direction as before but now with the hedge on the right. On the other side of the hedge is the Black Bourn. Ahead of you is the Pakenham windmill.

Pass on the left an old pit and join a cart track from the pit area into a lane with a bank on the left and trees on the right. At the lane end meet the road at Grimstone End, at a bend close to Baileypool Bridge. Go straight ahead and soon come to a T-junction and a grassy triangle. Here go a little bit to the right of straight ahead. Keep on along this quiet road through Grimstone End and you will come to Pakenham Water mill on your left.

Continue on along the road (north-west) until you reach the Ixworth bypass. The tarmac footway on the left leads you round to the road edge, and straight opposite is the end of another tarmac footway. Cross over this new by-pass with care, and go between the black and white posts that now close off the old road.

A short distance along this road takes you to a T-junction. Go right and so back towards Ixworth. Cross the Black Bourn once more and at the road junction in the village go straight ahead towards the church, and back to the car park.

Historical Notes

Ixworth: There was a major settlement here in Roman times. A Roman fort, a villa and pottery kilns have been found. Ixworth lay on the road the Romans built from London through Chelmsford, Long Melford, then through Ixworth to the Peddars Way and thence to the Wash.

Just outside Ixworth, about 1 mile to the south-east, alongside Stow Lane, a Roman building was found in 1834. It was discovered to be an extensive area of development, with a fairly sophisticated hypocaust heating system.

Ixworth Abbey: A private house within which is much that remains of the priory, in which once lived a prior and about 14 canons before the Dissolution in the reign of Henry VIII.

Pakenham: This is the only village in Britain now to have both a working water-mill and a working windmill. The water-mill is open to visitors at times (to check, ring Suffolk Preservation Society on Lavenham (0787) 247179). The windmill was built in 1831.

St Mary's Church: The octagonal tower is amidships on the crossing, not, as is more usual, at the west end. Pevsner says that this is decidedly rare in Suffolk. In the south-west corner of the church is the pedigree of the Pakenham family, of whom Lord Longford is the present head.

On the walls are some tributes to loving parents: '. . . she left an only daughter by a former husband who pays this tribute of affection to the memory of the best of mothers and most kind and indulgent stepfather.' Framed on the wall is a delightful map of Pakenham with many small watercolours of salient points in the village.

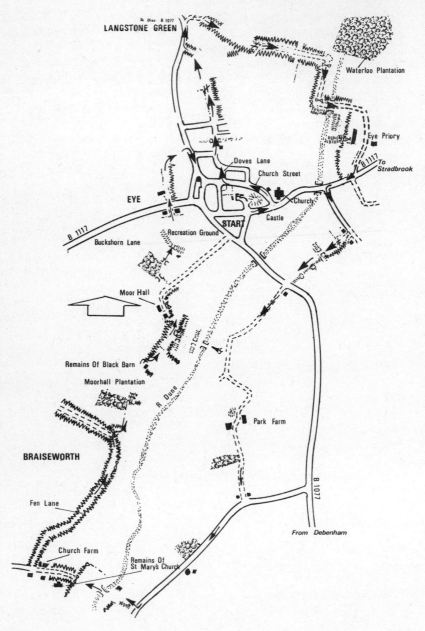

Eye and Braiseworth

Introduction: Eye is a small market town in the north of Suffolk, serving a wide rural community. It is now fortunately away from the main road, which preserves its charm. This walk starts in the centre of Eye, loops round the town, passing the castle, the church and the old guildhall, and extends both to the north and south of the town along the valley of the river Dove. The walk reaches into the parish of Braiseworth in the south.

Distance: This circular walk is 6 miles, and will take about 2½ hours. For those wishing to take a shorter walk, there is a short cut after about 2 miles, cutting out the southern loop to Braiseworth. Maps: OS Landranger 156, Pathfinder TM 07/17.

Refreshments: There are several choices in Eye, including The White Lion Hotel, Dove House café and the Queen's Head.

How to get there: Eye, which is near to the Norfolk/Suffolk border, is most easily approached from the Ipswich to Norwich road, (A140). Turn east from the A140 at Thornham Parva on to the B1117, or at Brome on to the B1077. Once in the main street of Eye (B1077) look out for the Victorian town hall on the west of the street. It is a prominent building. Turn east on to Church Street, almost opposite the Town Hall, and take the first turning to the right into Buckshorn Lane and thence to the car park, where the walk begins. Map ref: TM 146738.

The Walk: Leave the car park by a footpath in the far corner away from the road, leading to a flight of steps between two brick walls. At the top of the steps go under a canopy between buildings and out to a road in the centre of some very attractive modern houses in the shadow of Eye Castle.

Follow the road and at the end of the decorative brick road surface, you have on the left the gate to Eye Castle. (A notice on the gate tells where the key can be obtained if the gate is shut.) Continue on the road and at a crossroads turn left towards a beech tree. You will pass on the right a white house with an attractive entrance porch, and on the left an old house with Flemish gables.

Turn left into Church Street, passing St Peter and St Paul's Church, the Red Lion, and then the exit from the car park. Turn right opposite St Lukes House and go down Doves Lane.

At the end of Doves Lane turn left on to a road which soon swings right. You will see a brick wall on the left. Where the road turns left and at the end of the brick wall, turn right along a narrow tarmac footpath. Pass a small building, a pumping station on the right and go over a little bridge.

Soon you join a road, and a little further on, come to a T-junction with Ash Drive and 30 yards further on meet Ash Drive again. Here continue straight on, on a grassy path. Soon the path lies between a hedge on the right and the rear gardens of houses on the left. Pass a footpath (signed) on the right and at the end of the gardens on the left, go over a stile and continue for a few yards following a hedge on the right. Where the hedge ends, head half left to the corner of the field. You should make for a point to the right of a prominent house with a pyramid-shaped roof and go out between garden hedges to the road at Langstone Green and turn right.

As the road bears left just before the de-restriction sign, take the path half-right marked 'Private road to Brome Hall' and 'Eye Bowling Club'. Walk a few yards and turn right along a gravel track. Immediately leave the track which swings left into the bowls club and go straight on following a sunken lane between hedges. In a short distance, the green lane ends and you are in a field. Follow the high hedge on the right.

The hedge has a dog-leg bend to the left but you go straight on through a gap in the hedge into a lane with hedges on both sides. In about 200 yards go under electricity power lines and continue along the lane which, by a large concrete hard standing, and near some woods, Waterloo Plantation, turns right. Go through a gate into a field and follow the cart track with a hedge on the right. At the end of the field, go through a gate and turn left into a lane, which leads in about 50 yards to a bridge.

Go over the bridge and continue towards a stile beside a farm gate, near a house. Climb over the stile and curve round to the right along a concrete farm track. Follow this track, past cattle sheds to the right, later with the farmhouse to the left, on along the farm drive till you join a road.

You are now at a point where the drive from Abbey Farm meets the B1117. There is a gravel track opposite leading to Church Farm. Here turn right along the road towards Eye. (If you wish to curtail the walk, then continue along this road over Abbey Bridge to Eye Church from where you can retrace your steps to the car park.)

In about 50 yards there is a narrow road on the left. Turn left into the narrow road. Keep on the road for about 300 yards, passing some cottages on the right and you will reach a modernised house with a brick garden wall fronting the road. Immediately beyond the wall turn right.

Do not go up into the garden of the house (No. 5) but continue with the hedge on the left through a piece of very rough ground and then over a stile into a paddock. Still follow the hedge on the left. At the end of the paddock, cross a fence on to a grassy track beyond. From this point there is a bank with some isolated trees on the left. In about 300 yards reach the B1077 road to Debenham.

Go straight over the road and follow the gravel cart track opposite, passing a bungalow on the left. At first there are hedges on both sides, then just a bank on the left. This track then curves slowly round to the left. At about the beginning of the bend a hedge starts on the right. Continue along this lane. There is now a hedge on the right and scrub on the left. At the junction of tracks, swing round to the left on the main track. The track continues. It is almost a green lane with occasional trees and intermittent hedge on both sides. After a bend to the right, the track leads to Park Farm. At the farm pass a pond on the right and swing right and left through the farmyard, and continue on the track which is now a concrete drive with a hedge on the right. The hedge on the right shortly disappears and is replaced by a ditch with one or two isolated trees. After passing between two bungalows, you reach a road.

Turn right along the road. In about ¼ mile, pass Clint Farm on the left and go down the hill for about another ¼ mile to reach, on the right the first cross hedge after Clint Farm. Notice half left in the distance the aerial mast at Mendlesham. Turn right along the cross hedge and at the field boundary go through a gap between the hedge and some scrub into a long field stretching away to the left. Bear right and go round the end of the field to a wooden footbridge over the river Dove. Cross the bridge, and go through a gate to enter a field.

On the opposite side of the field are two gates. Make for the left-hand one which leads into a grassy green lane. Go up the lane and in about 200 yards, pass on the left an old churchyard and the remains of the former St Mary's Church. Keep straight on and go through Church Farm.

About 100 yards beyond the farm buildings and opposite a small colour-washed cottage turn right into a narrow green lane called Fen Lane, with a thick hedge on both sides. You follow this lane for about ½ mile. It can be overgrown and the path becomes narrow in parts. At first it veers to the right and then to the left. Eventually the lane, grassy underfoot, comes out into a very wide cart track with hedges on both sides. Here turn right and leave the lane, going through a gate at the end of the cart track and into a field.

Follow the hedge on the left for about 50 yards and then turn left at the internal corner of a field and follow the fence on the left. Pass on the left the end of Moorhall Plantation, then cross a stile without a footpiece and go over the footbridge.

You are now in a large field. Facing the same direction as you have been travelling, observe in the far distance some farm buildings. Make your way across the field towards the left hand end of the buildings. You will soon be able to identify the remaining walls, about 5 feet high, all that is left of Black Barn, one field away. Make for the left hand side of the barn and at the far end of the brick wall, cross a stile without a footpiece into a meadow and follow the hedge on your left. Go through a Suffolk gate and then continue to follow the hedge on your left as it swings round to the left. Here a path joins from the right. Continue to follow the hedge on the left and pass Moor Hall on the left. At the far left corner of this field go over the two-step stile and join the farm drive, and continue towards the town. You can see Eye Church half right.

The lane curves round to the right and about 50 yards from the bend, you turn left onto a well-trodden footpath. There is a fence on the right with some willow trees. The footpath leads over a concrete plank bridge into a poplar grove where you immediately turn half right towards the town. When you leave the poplars go over a wooden plank bridge and a little further on, another larger bridge into the recreation ground. Make your way across the recreation ground towards the children's play area and go out to the road by the left hand side of a prominent three-storey building.

Cross the road and follow the footpath sign, keeping the hedge on your right and the former railway station, now a factory, on the left. Keep on the tarmac footpath. At the end of the tarmac go straight on on a grassy footpath, with a hedge on the right and a fence on the left. When the fence ends and there are woods on the left, continue for about 30 yards, then the path swings to the right and you reach a road opposite an old white house.

You are now on the B1077 just north of Eye Town Square. Turn right, and pass the fire station. Opposite the Victorian Town Hall, turn left into Church Street and then first right into Buckshorn Lane, back to the car park where the walk began.

Historical Notes

Eye: The men of Heya, or Eya, had in the time of King John been granted a charter. In the reign of Queen Elizabeth I representatives of the people of Eye obtained a list of the previous charters from the Lord Keeper of the Great Seal. Among these documents was included in full a copy of the charter given by King John to Heya. It appears that in the days of King John the spelling of Eye, Suffolk, and Hythe, Kent, were very similar. The copy of the charter which the Eye men received is identical to the charter which Hythe, Kent was granted. It includes the rights to shipwrecks!

Eye Church: In the church of St Peter and St Paul William Honyng lies buried. His helmet had been hanging above his tomb since he died in 1569. In 1977 it was stolen by a 16-year-old Belgian youth who sold it to an Antwerp antique dealer for £250. Its actual worth at that time was £30,000. It was returned to England by the Belgian police.

WALK EIGHT

Eye Castle: The Normans built a castle at Eye. Not a great deal remains today of that castle, but you may walk to the top of the mound to enjoy the view.

The Broads at Beccles

Introduction: Few people realise that the extensive network of navigable waterways known as the Norfolk Broads, reach into Suffolk. Beccles is situated on high land overlooking the river Waveney at the southern extremity of the Broads. The enjoyment of the river is not limited to those who hire boats to sail its waters in the summer. The walker on the riverside paths will also delight in the changing views of the river as it meanders through the valley. This walk starts in the centre of Beccles, passes the quay where the river craft berth, and follows the river downstream for nearly 4 miles along part of the Angles Way, a regional trail along the Waveney Valley. From North Cove Staithe, the route of the walk goes south leaving the river and making a circuit round the town.

Distance: The full walk is 12 miles. The walk along the Waveney to North Cove, returning directly to Beccles is 8½ miles. Maps: OS Landranger 156 and 134, Pathfinder TM 48/58 and TM 49/59.

Refreshments: Beccles is well supplied with cafés, public houses and hotels. The Three Horseshoes public house at North Cove is a convenient halfway stop on the walk.

How to get there: Beccles is on the Suffolk-Norfolk border. Coming from the south, use the main A12 London to Lowestoft road to just north of Blythburgh, where you turn left onto the A145 for Beccles. From the west, use the A143 Bury St Edmunds to Great Yarmouth road. At Bungay follow the signs to Beccles. The starting point of the walk is the parish church in the centre of the town. Parking is available at the Pay and Display car park off Blyburgate. Map ref: TM 421905.

The Walk: The walk starts from St Michael's Church, right in the

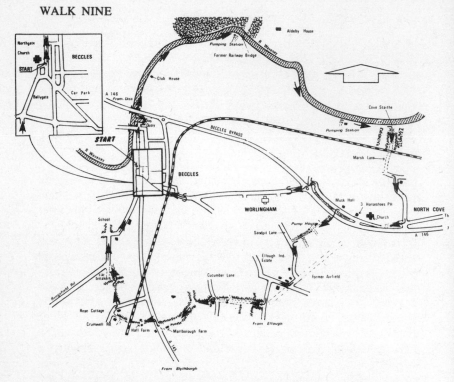

centre of Beccles. Go north away from the shops, and pass the end of Puddingmoor, close by St Peter's House Hotel.

Continue along Northgate to the crossroads. You will see on your left at this point the bridge over the Waveney. Keep straight on along Fen Lane and you will come to the Quay. Go a few yards to the right and cross this spur of the Waveney by a wooden footbridge, and turn left beside the water. Follow round and go under the Beccles by-pass, which was opened in 1982.

The route follows the river bank for just over 3½ miles. Two red triangles on white posts, facing the river, record the beginning and end of a measured quarter-mile. Presently you will pass a brick pumping station, held together with a great many tie-rods. About 50 yards after the pump-house a path goes off right over a wooden cart-bridge towards a cross-paths. That is not on your route. You go about a yard to the left and then on, following the river bank. A bit further on still are several dark-blue brick piers, some to the right, some to the left and one in midstream which carries a navigation light. This is the site of a railway swing bridge.

Do not turn off where there is a sign facing the river saying 'Broads Authority Free Mooring for 24 hours only', but keep on beside the river. Cross a Y-shaped concrete footbridge and pass a small red-brick pumping station. There is a matching one on the other side of the river, 200 yards further on.

Shortly after passing the end of a long narrow belt of poplars, you will come to a large notice about North Cove and Barnby Angling Club Water which faces a lane on the right. You are now at Cove Staithe.

At this point leave the river, dropping down right, over a wooden cart-bridge into a green lane, lined with many mature trees. This green lane is called Cove Dam. Keep straight on until you come to a level crosing. Cross by the long white kissing-gates.

The road you are now on, Marsh Lane, curves round until you come to a T-junction. You go right for North Cove. Continue on this road until you join Pinewood Gardens at a T-junction, turn right and very soon reach a junction, off left, The Street. You are now within sight of the A146 Beccles to Lowestoft road, as it bypasses North Cove village.

At this T-junction you go right, along the old road, now shut off to traffic but a pleasant, leafy, quiet road to walk along. You come soon to the Three Horseshoes public house, North Cove, standing close by North Cove Church. Continue along the old road until you have just passed the great iron entrance gates to Musk Hall on your right.

(At this point those wishing to return directly to Beccles should continue straight on. The old road which you are on will join the main road at a roundabout. Cross the main road and take the road to Worlingham which will lead back to Beccles.)

A few yards further on go through a gap in the hedge on the left and cross, with great care, the main road, to a footpath sign just opposite.

Follow the power lines, and later a line of poplars on your right. Pass on your right a pump house and ancillary works, then cross a gravel farm track with grass in the middle.

Keep straight on, ditch on right. Away on your left across the field is Sprite's Wood. Cross a ditch running to your left, by a culvert. From this, the third field since the road, you can see huddles of buildings some distance away on what was once an airfield. Leave this third field by a wide gap and a footpath sign to meet a minor road, Sandpit Lane, and turn left.

Pass the old airfield buildings and your road soon meets the old runway, now a road, at a wide junction. Turn right and in 300 more yards reach another T-junction, where again you go right. Walk along this road, Benacre Road, with its broad green verges, passing one access road on each side, until you reach a T-junction to the left, signposted 'ELLOUGH'. Go left here, and with a single power line overhead continue until you come to a lane off to the right, where three wires cross the road.

Turn into the lane which has hedges on both sides. Continue straight on. The lane gets narrower, soon you go through a small three-bar metal gate which leads into a narrow path.

Soon you join a road at a corner, where a pink-washed cottage is on the other side. This is Cucumber Lane. Go right along the road for a few yards, and shortly after passing a transformer on a pole on the right of the road, turn off the road to the left along a green lane, about 30 yards long.

Continue with hedge on right in a westerly direction. Half-left you can see Weston Church nestling in a shallow valley. At the end of the field go through a gap and join another green lane, at a Y-junction. Go to the left and almost immediately the track curves round to the right. As you approach some newish buildings around Marlborough Farm on the left, there is a row of conifers just before you emerge onto a road opposite a house. There is a bridleway signpost here.

Turn right and follow the A145 until the road swings right. That will be when within sight of a couple of cottages on the right of the road.

Just here go left off the road by the footpath sign, along a gravel drive to Hall Farm. At the end there are buildings to both left and right. When you reach the house, on your right, go to the left of the line of poplars ahead. With those poplars on your right pass a wooden shed on your right, and then a cross-hedge on your left. Keep a hedge on your right all the way to the two-step railway stile. Cross the railway at this skew-crossing with great care and go over the other white railway stile.

Go left a yard or two towards a fence and then turn right and follow the fence on left, hedge on right, north-west, along the narrow path until you join the drive of the house on your left. Pass the cottages of Paradise Row on your left and join the Cromwell Road.

Turn right along the road. The road swings right and just beyond Rose Villas, where a wooden fence on the left begins, you turn left off the road along the path between a hedge and barbed wire fence.

Pass through a cross-hedge on the left, and continue still with a hedge on the right. Presently there is a car breakers' yard, screened behind trees; here snake right a yard and continue with hedge on the left. Later as you approach a line of poplars swing left, join a concrete drive by the entrance gates of the breakers' yard, and with poplars on your right walk out to the road.

Go right along the Ringsfield Road, passing Barnaby Farm on your left, and later, on the right an official-looking building and then a field which will probably have some very fearsome-looking bulls in it.

Follow the road round a sharp bend to the right, and then left, passing the fairly modern Sir John Leman High School. At the crossroads you will see the Beccles Town Sign, showing the Port Reeve receiving the Charter of 1584 from Queen Elizabeth I.

Follow ancient Ballygate, passing several 'scores', as the pedestrian ways here are called, leading down to Puddingmoor, another very old street, and to the river beyond. Ballygate will lead you back to your start at St Michael's Church.

Historical Notes

Beccles: The Parish Church of St Michael, was for the most part built in the fourteenth century. On May 11th, 1749 the curate of St Michael's Church was married in that church. He, the Rev. Edmund Nelson, married Catherine Suckling. In 1758 they had a son, a son of whom all England knows: Horatio.

Around the year 1700 Beccles was the third largest town in Suffolk, after Ipswich and Bury St Edmunds. The town has two market places; even the one known as New Market was in existence in the thirteenth century.

The Beccles Society has published an excellent booklet called *Exploring Beccles* and copies can be bought in the town. It gives a commentary on the historic houses passed en route.

River Waveney: Much hemp was grown in the Waveney Valley in the nineteenth century. At one time there were over 100 looms in operation in the valley. The river is navigable as far as Beccles, and at one time Norfolk Wherries would be a common sight at the quay.

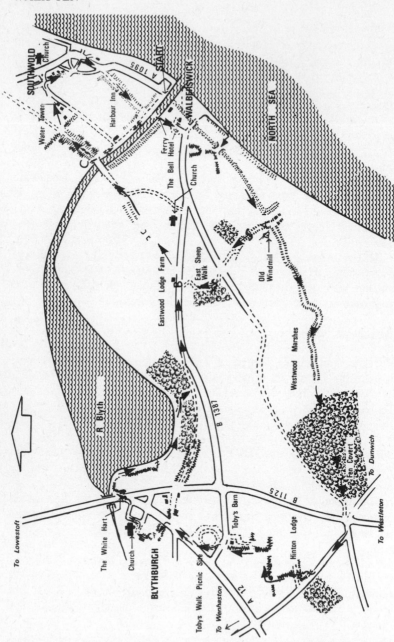

Southwold, Walberswick and Blythburgh

Introduction: Southwold is a delightful seaside town, with a number of greens. The river Blyth flows out to the sea here, and the narrow river estuary forms the harbour which is used by a variety of small sea-going craft. Inland from the harbour, the estuary widens out to form a broad shallow tidal lake extending to the village of Blythburgh. The land to the south of the Blyth is a mixture of marsh, heathland and woods, as well as some farmland.

The walk starts at the harbour. You cross the river by ferry and after a short distance along the shore, you traverse the marshes through the nature reserve. Thence across farmland to Blythburgh, with its large and famous church.

The return to the harbour generally follows the route of the former light railway alongside the estuary, and goes through another part of the nature reserve and back to the harbour.

Distance: This circular walk is 12 miles and will take about 5-5½ hours. For a shorter walk of 6 miles you can cut across East Sheep Walk as shown on the sketch map. Maps: OS Landranger 156, Pathfinder TM 47/57.

Refreshments: There are a number of public houses, cafés and restaurants in both Southwold and Walberswick. The following are on, or close to the route: The Bell Hotel, Walberswick, The Anchor Hotel, Walberswick, The White Hart, Blythburgh and the Harbour Inn, Southwold Harbour.

How to get there: Southwold is on the coast. Turn east off the main A12 Lowestoft to London road, just north of Blythburgh, onto the A1095. Keep on this road, which swings right at the centre of Southwold, and in about ¾ mile reach the harbour. The starting

continue clockwise until you reach a fenced enclosure on the left. Follow the fence out to the left to join the main road.

The main road is the A12 London to Lowestoft road. Turn right and walk down the busy road, with care, for about 400 yards. Pass on your left the road to Wenhaston, and pass on your right, just before the first house, a footpath which would lead back to Walberswick. In about 50 yards, and opposite the drive to a house called 'Hillside', turn left off the road along a narrow path. At the end of the path, about 30 yards, turn right over a stile into a long meadow. Make towards the church and some white cottages, keeping the hedge on your left. When you reach the cottages, go left about a yard and then right over a stile and up the lane to the church.

Go through the churchyard keeping the church on your left, and leave the churchyard at the north-east corner by a bend in the road. Follow the road, away from the church, passing the Priory on the left to reach the main road, where you turn left. In a few yards, pass the White Hart public house on the right. Cross the road, and just beyond the White Hart, take the lane on the right leading almost parallel to the main road.

At the end of the lane, turn right, go up some steps and over a stile. You are on the river wall with the wide expanse of the Blyth estuary on your left. Continue on this path for about a mile. This path lies in the main along the route of the former Southwold railway.

Along this path you enter the Walberswick Nature Reserve. About ¾ mile from Blythburgh, leaving the river, you start to climb slightly, with woods on your left. At a junction of paths where there is a notice saying 'No Entry on Foot — Horse Riders Only', turn right, dropping down a slight bank and in about 30 yards meet a well-defined track. Turn left.

Walk straight on on this wide bridleway across rough heathland, and in due course the path comes out to a road. This is the B1387 road to Walberswick. Continue along the road for about ½ mile. Pass on the left some farmbuildings. Then, just after passing the first house on the left by some scots pines, take the path to the left. It is signposted 'Bridleway Walberswick', and is the point where those who took the cut across East Sheep Walk rejoin the main route.

You are now on a well-used grassy track across rough pasture called Walberswick Common. Go straight on at a cross paths.

Further on at a junction of paths, go through a gate and continue straight on. Note to the left the abutments of a former railway bridge. You will also see the railway embankment, and further on, a cutting on the left. This grassy path meets at a T-junction, a narrow tarmac track, almost a road. Here the bridleway to Walberswick goes right, but you go left along the tarmac. The way swings right and follows the line of the former railway. Follow the path slightly downhill to reach the bridge over the river Blyth.

If you want to take the shortest route to the starting point, turn right now and follow the north bank of the river, back to the car park.

Continuing the main walk to Southwold, cross the river bridge and continue along the tarmac track. At the point where the meadows on either side give way to heathland on rising ground, the tarmac surfacing ends. There is a signpost here reading, to the right 'Footpath over common to Town Centre'. Turn right towards the town.

Pass on the right the clubhouse and the tennis court, but keep on the higher ground. You are now crossing the golf course. The path passes very close to two water towers. At the base of the old water tower is the Southwold R.N.L.I. Lifeboat Museum (open daily 2.30 to 4.30). Having passed the water towers on your right, join the road which leads from the harbour and keep straight on.

On reaching the houses at the edge of the common, turn right and follow Godyll Road, skirting the town and keeping the common on your right. (If you wish to visit the church and the shops, do not turn into Godyll Road, but keep straight on.)

You will eventually reach a public car park on the right and just beyond, is a five-way junction. Go straight ahead into Lorne Road and at the end of Lorne Road, turn right. You will be opposite the Red Lion public house. Walk down the green with several large houses on both sides and the sea 100 yards away on the left.

At the bottom of the hill and at the edge of the marshes and meadows of the river valley, the road swings left and another road comes in obliquely from the right. As the road swings left into Ferry Road, go straight on along a narrow lane lying to the right of Ferry Road. Pass an old building labelled Southwold Town Council. The lane becomes narrower. There is a bank on the left and a watercourse on the right. In about ½ mile, climb the river wall and you will be at Southwold Harbour, almost opposite the ferry landing stage. Turn left, back to the car park.

Historical Notes

Southwold: Southwold was a small fishing community in Saxon times, and by the time the Domesday Book was compiled was required to pay 25,000 herrings to Bury St Edmunds. Non-observance of fast days after the Reformation and increased piracy on the seas seriously affected the fishing industry.

At the height of the herring fishing industry's prosperity the Board of Trade wanted to use Southwold to relieve the congestion at Great Yarmouth and Lowestoft. In 1908 the harbour was again busy exporting thousands of barrels of cured fish.

In 1659 fire devastated the town. In four hours the town was almost completely destroyed, and it was nearly a hundred years before its prosperity as a maritime town was restored.

Southwold Museum, in a quaint Dutch-style cottage opposite the church, has many exhibits of local interest.

Walberswick, now a small picturesque village on the southern side of the Blyth estuary, was once a prosperous and thriving place. The inhabitants relied on fishing and shipbuilding for their prosperity. This early prosperity may have been influenced by Walberswick's proximity to the ancient, and now lost, town of Dunwich.

Blythburgh: It is a small village but its magnificent church of the Holy Trinity is a landmark in the wide open landscape of the Blyth valley.

At one time 500 to 600 years ago Blythburgh was a port with quays and wharves but with the development of technology, vessels became larger, and trade to the new world developed and Blythburgh became unable to service the new ships.

In AD 654 a Christian Anglo-Saxon king Anna was slain in a battle against Mercia at Bulcamp nearby. His body was taken to a church on the site of the present Blythburgh church. The present church was built in the fifteenth century by workers from the nearby Priory. Modern history is recorded in the church by a small notice which states that Joseph Kennedy, the eldest brother of John F. Kennedy, former president of the U.S.A., was flying over the church on August 12th, 1944 in a U.S. aircraft when it blew up with 12 tons of explosives on board.

The Southwold Railway which opened in 1879 was a 3-foot narrow gauge light railway running between Halesworth and Southwold. It closed in 1929 because with its limited speed of 18mph it was unable to compete with a motorbus service to Southwold which could go at 20mph.

Acknowledgements:

We would express our thanks to all members of our family for encouragement and help, particularly in giving the walks a 'test run'.

Particular thanks are due to Mary Bird for help in research and Roger Pratt for assistance with the sketch maps.

Finally we acknowledge with thanks the information and help given regarding the Definitive Map by the Rights of Way staff and Area Wardens of the Suffolk County Council's Highways Department.

Jean and Geoff Pratt